"*One God, Shared Hope* reminds us once again that lasting truths are often expressed simply and directly. This beautiful book reveals an indisputable harmony between religions that prompts a reader's soul to wonder, 'Why is there anything but union among all people?'"

—Jeff Moses, author of *Oneness: Great Principles Shared by All Religions*

"*One God, Shared Hope* expresses its intention for peace and understanding clearly and eloquently. What unites us greatly outweighs what separates us when we listen with the ears of wisdom."

—Dr. Neil Douglas-Klotz (Saadi Shakur Chishti), author of *Original Meditation: A Shared Language of Peace* and *New Beginnings for Christians, Jews and Muslims*

"The front pages of newspapers give reasons for people of Jewish, Christian, and Islamic faiths to perpetuate hostilities. *One God, Shared Hope* provides a deep starting place to discover peace among the same people."

—The Rt. Rev. William E. Swing, Bishop, Episcopal Diocese of California

one god
shared hope

TWENTY

THREADS

SHARED BY

JUDAISM,

CHRISTIANITY,

AND ISLAM

MAGGIE OMAN SHANNON

Red Wheel
Boston, MA / York Beach, ME

First published in 2003 by
Red Wheel/Weiser, LLC
York Beach, ME
With offices at:
368 Congress Street
Boston, MA 02210
www.redwheelweiser.com

Library of Congress Cataloging-in-Publication Data

Oman Shannon, Maggie,
  One God, shared hope : twenty threads shared by Judaism,
Christianity, and Islam / Maggie Oman Shannon
      p. cm.
Includes bibliographical references.
    ISBN 1-59003-051-6 (pbk. : alk. paper)
    1. Koran—Relation to the Bible. 2. Islam—Relations—
Christianity. 3. Christianity and other religions—Islam 4. Islam—
Relations—Judaism. 5. Judaism—Relations—Islam. I. Title
  BP134.B4 O46 2003
    291.8'2—dc21

Typeset in Weiss by Gopa & Ted2

Printed in Canada

TCP

10 09 08 07 06 05 04 03
 8 7 6 5 4 3 2 1

This book is dedicated
with gratitude, respect, and admiration
to Angeles Arrien,
whose tireless work to bridge cultures
and cultivate peace—
and impeccable personal example—
contribute so much to so many.

contents

acknowledgments

First, I would like to thank Jan Johnson, who blessed me with the opportunity to develop her wonderful idea, which has turned into *One God, Shared Hope*. Thanks also to my agent, Tom Grady; and to the staff of Red Wheel/Weiser. I also want to acknowledge and thank all those people whose compilations preceded this work, including contemporary anthologists Timothy Freke (*The Illustrated Book of Sacred Scriptures*), Jeffrey Moses (Oneness: Great Principles Shared by All Religions), Philip Novak (*The World's Wisdom: Sacred Texts of the World's Religions*), and Andrew Wilson (World Scripture: A Comparitive Anthology of Sacred Texts). And we are all indebted to the messengers, translators, and editors of years past who have so invaluably aided our efforts today to develop a deeper understanding of one another's traditions.

Personally, I would like to thank my teacher and mentor Angeles Arrien, to whom this book is dedicated; as well as my husband, Scott Shannon, my mother, Jane Oman, and my brother, Carl Oman, for their love and support. Special thanks always to Molly Starr and the other wonderful women in my circle of friends for the gift of their precious presence.

Above all, I give thanks to the God of my understanding for the many blessings of my life. Having the opportunity to spend my workdays in further exploration of the Mystery is an awesome gift indeed, and I am so very grateful for this immense privilege.

introduction

While working on this book, I read a review of a book on Islam in which the author had compared the scriptures of Islam with those of Judaism and Christianity. In the review, the writer made the comment that the three religions are very different; that cases can be made to support those differences or the opposite; and that the scripture passages chosen in any effort of this sort say a great deal more about the person selecting them than they do about the religions from which they come.

If that be true, then it will be clear that this author holds an inherently positive outlook, and I will admit my personal bias at the onset: the belief that, as stated in 1 John 4:8, "God is love." I will leave it to others to make cases for the differences we face, and should delving into that be of interest to those reading this introduction, they won't have any problem finding such material. But it seems far more compelling, indeed urgent, to discover the similarities we have, to begin with what we share and what we hope for, to hold fast to our dreams for peace in the world—or to create them anew if we have never dared dream before.

This book is offered as one small link toward building a chain of understanding. Are some of the scriptural passages in this book taken out of context? Will the translations used affect some of the nuances of the original? By necessity, the answer to both questions is yes. Indeed, that has been one of the intrinsic ironies of attempting a collection of this sort; the realization that what we are looking at here are representations. Like phyllo dough, our scriptures are a construction of parchment, layers of translations occurring in layers of time, providing us with something now that may be best approached by both the mind and the heart.

The reader is invited to look at the following scriptures for their spirit, even for their metaphor, when encountering words that can provoke a reaction in today's sophisticated, often jaded, world—words like "evil" and "sin," as well as language that is not gender-inclusive. While you may, as I did, find many strings of resonant words that touch your heart deeply, a twenty-first-century perspective can sometimes be a problematic filter for ancient injunctions. At those times, it might be helpful to look at them as "not of the letter, but of the Spirit" (2 Corinthians 3:6).

Taking this one step further, it is important to note that Muslims consider any translation of the Koran *not* the Koran, as the Koran was given to Muhammad in Arabic. For this reason, Muslims of every nationality learn Arabic in order to read what they believe is the true Koran. And readers of the scriptures of Judaism and Christianity also know that different versions involve different word choices in their translations. All of this clearly makes any comparison of scriptures inexact at best.

Yet these challenges shouldn't negate the value of beginning the search to see what principles we share as revealed by our holy scriptures; thus this book is offered as a place to begin a journey that could take a lifetime. I hope that readers will approach it as a marker on the path; a signpost that invites people to explore this trail, or that. For this reason, I have included the numeric references where people will find these passages, so that they can continue their own exploration.

One other note: When researching this book, I expanded my frame of reference to include the Talmud, the rabbinical teachings about the laws and ethics of Judaism, as well as the Hadith, the collected sayings of Muhammad that elucidate elements of the Koran. Because there is no real equivalent for these in the Christian tradition—and because there are varying levels of authority and import assigned to these writings within their own traditions—I ultimately chose not to include a large sampling of teachings from the Talmud or Hadith in these pages. While I highly recommend both of these teachings as important to include in one's own exploration, it seemed appropriate here to focus more exclusively on the recognized scriptures themselves. I have listed the passages in the order of their religious and historic chronology; thus the scriptures of

Judaism (known and embraced by Christians as the Old Testament) are followed by those of Christianity, which are followed by those of Islam.

To aid the reader, I have standardized pronouns, changing any "thees" and "thines" to "you" and "yours." I have also eliminated some capitalizations. Additionally, to again place all of these faith traditions on a more level field of understanding, the word "God" has been used in all instances. Since "Allah" is the Arabic word for "God," Jews and Christians who speak Arabic would use the word "Allah" in worship. Thus, for our purposes, reading these verses in English, the word "God" is used in all passages. Sources for all the quotations can be found in the "Resources for Further Study" section.

~

In summary, I can think of no better words to quote than the Dalai Lama's, who wrote the following in his introduction to my first book, *Prayers for Healing*: "I believe it is essential that we extend our understanding of each other's spiritual practices and prayers. This is not necessarily in order that we can adopt them ourselves, but because to do so increases our opportunities for mutual respect. Sometimes, too, we encounter something in another tradition that helps us better appreciate something in our own."

Both of these experiences have held true for me in the course of working on *One God, Shared Hope*. Poring over the ancient words of people many centuries removed, I have been touched and sometimes moved to tears by the beauty, wisdom, and earnestness of passages I found in the scriptures and teachings of each of these religions. At the same time, I have also drawn closer to my own faith tradition—or perhaps it would be more accurate to say, my own faith tradition drew me back to it.

And that is my prayer for all readers of this book: both that our hearts might be filled with appreciation and respect for the faith traditions of others, and that we might draw closer to our own. For as faith-filled people, we do indeed share hope. And as faith-filled people, we know that we have the power of God to draw upon— that we not only can share hope, but can collectively create a shared future.

In the thirteenth century, the Sufi poet Rumi wrote, "Out beyond ideas of wrongdoing and rightdoing, there is a field. I'll meet you there." May we heed his wisdom today and become willing to expand our capacities for understanding. May we suspend our ideas of wrongdoing and rightdoing long enough to meet on our common ground. May God help us to create peace in our hearts and to work for peace in our world.

How good and pleasant it is when brothers live together in unity!
—Psalms 133:1

~

*That all of them may be one, Father, just as you are in me,
and I am in you.... May they be brought to complete unity.* —John 17:21

~

*And truly this Brotherhood of yours is a single Brotherhood.
And I am your Lord and Cherisher.* —Koran 23:54

the principles
concerning god

1. worship and praise god

It all starts here, with the "In the beginning" of Genesis 1:1 ("In the beginning God created the heavens and the earth") and the first *surah* of the Koran (1:1–5): "In the name of God, most gracious, most merciful, praise be to God, the cherisher and sustainer of the worlds; most gracious, most merciful master of the day of judgment. You do we worship, and your aid we seek." We, as Jews and Christians and Muslims, are "People of the Book," all descended from Abraham. We worship God, and we love to praise God, for from God originates everything.

Yours, O Lord, is the greatness and the power, and the glory and the majesty and the splendor; for everything in heaven and earth is yours.
—1 Chronicles 29:11

For Him all things were created: things in heaven and on earth, visible and invisible, whether thrones or powers or rulers or authorities; all things were created by Him and for Him. —Colossians 1:16

To Him belong the most beautiful names; whatever is in the heavens and on earth does declare His praises and glory. —Koran 59:24

And worship is something that all of creation participates in, for in God we all "live and move and have our being" (Acts 17:28).

All you have made will praise you, O Lord; your saints will extol you. They will tell of the glory of your kingdom. —Psalms 145:10–11

Worship the Lord in the splendor of His holiness; tremble before Him, all the earth. —Psalms 96:9

Christ is all, and is in all. —Colossians 3:11

See you not that it is God whose praises all beings in the heavens and on earth do celebrate, and the birds of the air with wings outspread? —Koran 24:41

And how is it that we are to worship God? For Jews, it is practicing the Shema; for Muslims, the *Shahadah*: proclamations that, sim-
ilar to the Christian's Nicene Creed, are fervent statements of faith.
But even before the proclamation of faith comes the movement of
the heart.

*Love the Lord your God with all your heart and with all your soul
and with all your strength.* —Deuteronomy 6:5

*Love the Lord your God with all your heart and with all your soul
and with all your mind and with all your strength.* —Mark 12:30

*O you who believe! Celebrate the praises of God, and do so often;
and glorify Him morning and evening. He it is Who sends blessings on you,
as do His angels, that He may bring you out from the depths of darkness
into light.* —Koran 33:42–43

And what exactly is worship of God?

Stop and consider God's wonders. —Job 37:14

Be still, and know that I am God. —Psalms 46:10

Come, let us bow down in worship: let us kneel before the Lord our maker.
—Psalms 95:6

I will extol the Lord at all times; his praise will always be on my lips.
—Psalms 34:1

*Yet a time is coming and has now come when the true worshipers will
worship the Father in spirit and truth; for they are the kind of worshipers
the Father seeks.* —John 4:23

~

Worship can also be done with great joy.

*Praise him with the sounding of the trumpet; praise him with the harp and the
lyre, praise him with the tambourine and dancing; praise him with the strings
and flute, praise him with the clash of cymbals.* —Psalms 150:3–5

This is the day the Lord has made; let us rejoice and be glad in it.
—Psalms 118:24

~

And who is this God that we worship?

God said to Moses, "I AM WHO I AM." —Exodus 3:14

The eternal God is your refuge. —Deuteronomy 33:27

I am the Alpha and the Omega, the beginning and the end.
—Revelation 21:6

I am the way and the truth and the life. —John 14:6

He is God, the Creator, the Evolver, the Bestower of Forms or Colors.
To him belong the most beautiful names: whatever is in the heavens
and on earth declares His praises and glory; and He is the Exalted in might,
the Wise. —Koran 59:24

2. read the scriptures

The importance of reading the sacred scriptures of our faith is stressed in each of our traditions, as the scriptures have been given to us by God for instruction and guidance.

Blessed is the man who does not walk in the counsel of the wicked ...
but his delight is in the law of the Lord: and on his law he meditates day
and night. —Psalms 1:1–2

If you hold to my teaching, you are really my disciples. Then you will
know the truth, and the truth will set you free. —John 8:31–32

Instruct them in Scripture and wisdom, and sanctify them: for You are
the Exalted in might, the Wise. —Koran 2:129

Our approach to the scriptures should be one of reverence; by meditating upon holy passages and loving their laws, we are changed. The scriptures become part of our minds and hearts.

I desire to do your will, O my God; your law is within my heart.
—Psalms 40:8

Oh, how I love your law! I meditate on it all day long. —Psalms 119:97

If anyone loves me, he will obey my teaching. My Father will love him, and we will come to him and make our home with him. —John 14:23

When the Qur'an is read, listen to it with attention.... Bring your Lord to remembrance in your very soul. —Koran 7:204–5

Yet we are to use what we learn, to put it into practice.

Therefore everyone who hears these words of mine and puts them into practice is like a wise man who built his house on the rock. —Matthew 7:24

Do not merely listen to the word, and so deceive yourselves. Do what it says. —James 1:22

Those who rehearse the Book of God, establish regular prayer, and spend in charity out of what We have provided for them, secretly and openly, hope for a Commerce that will never fail. —Koran 35:29

If we follow the guidance of our God, we are blessed and protected.

Great peace have they who love Your law, and nothing can make
them stumble. —Psalms 119:165

But the man who looks intently into the perfect law that brings freedom,
and continues to do this, not forgetting what he has heard, but doing it—
he will be blessed in what he does. —James 1:25

When you read the Qur'an, seek God's protection from Satan the rejected one.
No authority has he over those who believe and put their trust in their Lord.
—Koran 16:98–99

We see our Scriptures as being the words of God, as being Truth.

The tablets were the work of God; the writing was the writing of God, engraved on the tablets. —Exodus 32:16

I will tell you what is written in the Book of Truth. —Daniel 10:21

No prophecy of scripture came about by the prophet's own interpretation. For prophecy never had its origin in the will of man, but men of God spoke as they were carried along by the Holy Spirit. —2 Peter 1:20–21

To you We sent the Scripture in Truth, confirming the scripture that came before it, and guarding it in safety. —Koran 5:48

~

Yet we are to be active with our Scriptures; in it are the answers to our deepest questions.

Your word is a lamp to my feet and a light for my path. —Psalms 119:105

From infancy you have known the holy scriptures, which are able to make you wise for salvation ... all scripture is God-breathed, and is useful for teaching, rebuking, correcting and training in righteousness. —2 Timothy 3:15–16

Those to whom we have sent the Book study it as it should be studied—
they are the ones that believe therein; those who reject faith therein—
the loss is their own. —Koran 2:115

~

Whatever else we might believe about our scriptures, we know
that they will be part of our lives always.

The grass withers and the flowers fall, but the word of our God stands forever.
—Isaiah 40:8

Heaven and earth will pass away, but my words will never pass away.
—Mark 13:31

It is a Book of exalted power. No falsehood can approach it from before
or behind it. It is sent down by One full of wisdom, worthy of all praise.
—Koran 41:41–42

3. release other idols (distractions)

By very definition, the three major monotheistic religions of Judaism, Christianity, and Islam follow the injunction found in Exodus 20:3: "You shall have no other gods before me." While our varying conceptions of God impact how we understand this commandment, it is the foundation of our Abrahamic traditions.

For great is the Lord and most worthy of praise; he is to be feared above all gods. —1 Chronicles 16:25

I am God, and there is no other. —Isaiah 45:22

It is written: "Worship the Lord your God, and serve only him."
—Matthew 4:10

Who has made the earth your couch and the heavens your canopy;
and sent down rain from the heavens; and brought forth therewith fruits
for your sustenance; then set not up rivals unto God when you know
the truth. —Koran 2:22

At the time in which these scriptures were written, believers were to follow the commandment to release idols literally, to cast away other objects of worship.

They sacrificed to demons, which are not God—gods they had not known.
—Deuteronomy 32:17

They became fools, and exchanged the glory of the immortal God for images made to look like mortal man and birds and animals and reptiles.
—Romans 1:22–23

Muslims take the admonition against idol-worship so seriously that Islamic religious art is not representative; the concern for them is that a visual representation would encourage *shirk*, the act of deifying something other than God.

For I desire mercy, not sacrifice, and acknowledgment of God rather than burnt offerings. —Hosea 6:6

Man-made gods are no gods at all. —Acts 19:26

Say: "I do no more than invoke My Lord, and I join not with Him any false god." —Koran 72:20

Yet even beyond this, we must choose where to place our attention. Idols can also be found in those things that distract us from God.

If you return to the Almighty, you will be restored: if you remove wickedness far from your tent and assign your nuggets to the dust, your gold of Ophir to the rocks in the ravines; then the Almighty will be your gold, the choicest silver for you. Surely then you will find delight in the Almighty and will lift up your face to God. —Job 22:23–26

Do not store up for yourselves treasures on earth, where moth and rust destroy, and where thieves break in and steal. But store up for yourselves treasures in heaven, where moth and rust do not destroy, and where thieves do not break in and steal. For where your treasure is, there your heart will be also. —Matthew 6:19–21

The material things which ye are given are but the conveniences of this life and the glitter thereof; but that which is with God is better and more enduring: Will ye not then be wise? —Koran 28:60

The reasons for being conscious of where we direct our attention
are made clear to us:

When you cry out for help, let your collection of idols save you!
The wind will carry all of them off, a mere breath will blow them away.
But the man who makes me his refuge will inherit the land and possess my
holy mountain. —Isaiah 57:13

No one can serve two masters. Either he will hate the one, and love the other, or
he will be devoted to the one and despise the other. —Matthew 6:24

God will not forgive that partners should be set up with Him; but He forgives
anything else, to whom He pleases; to set up partners with God is to devise
a sin most heinous indeed. —Koran 4:48

And lest we think that money, and the pursuit of it, is the only thing that is considered an obstacle in the path to God, we are given more possibilities to consider; our attitudes and our interests are also to be examined.

This is what the Lord says: Let not the wise man boast of his wisdom
or the strong man boast of his strength or the rich man boast of his riches,
but let him who boasts boast about this: that he understands and knows me,
for I am the Lord, who exercises kindness, justice, and righteousness on earth,
for in these I delight. —Jeremiah 9:22–24

For rebellion is like the sin of divination, and arrogance like the evil of idolatry.
—1 Samuel 15:23

Whatever belongs to your earthly nature: sexual immorality, impurity, lust,
evil desires and greed, which is idolatry. —Colossians 3:5

O you who believe! Intoxicants and gambling, dedication of stones, and
divination by arrows, an abomination. —Koran 5:92

O you who believe! What is the matter with you, that, when you are asked
to go forth in the cause of God, cling heavily to the earth? Do you prefer
the life of this world to the Hereafter? But little is the comfort of this life,
as compared to the Hereafter. —Koran 9:38

This admonition to avoid distractions relates as well to what our relationships are to be with the people in our world who hold power.

Be still, and know that I am God; I will be exalted among the nations, I will be exalted in the earth. —Psalms 46:10

Give to Caesar what is Caesar's, and to God what is God's.
—Matthew 22:21

God has said: Take not for worship two gods: for He is just one God.
—Koran 16:51

Though we must "Choose for yourselves this day whom you will serve" (Joshua 24:15), there are rewards for choosing God.

Blessed are those whose strength is in you. —Psalms 84:5

If you are returning to the Lord with all your hearts, then rid yourselves of the foreign gods ... and commit yourselves to the Lord and serve him only, and he will deliver you. —1 Samuel 7:3

But seek first [God's] kingdom and His righteousness, and all these things will be given to you as well. —Matthew 6:33

Remain in me, and I in you. —John 15:4

"There is no god but You: Glory to You: I was indeed wrong."
So We listened to him: and delivered him from distress: and thus do
We deliver those who have faith. —Koran 21:88–89

Whosoever believes in God has grasped the most trustworthy handhold, that never breaks. And God hears and knows all things. —Koran 2:256

4. be faithful and obedient

Given that our faith traditions each recognize us as descendants of Abraham, our paths begin here. Faithfulness and obedience are closely aligned; to have faith in God means that we are called to be obedient to God.

The Lord appeared to [Abraham], and said, "I am God Almighty; walk before me and be blameless." —Genesis 17:1

Fear God and keep His commandments, for this is the whole duty of man. —Ecclesiastes 12:13

If you love me, you will obey what I command. —John 14:15

But follow that which comes to you by inspiration from your Lord: for God is well acquainted with all that you do. And put your trust in God. —Koran 33:2–3

By obeying God, we are able to demonstrate our faithfulness and devotion.

To obey is better than sacrifice, and to heed is better than the fat of rams.
—1 Samuel 15:22

Praise the Lord. Blessed is the man who fears the Lord, who finds great delight in his commands. —Psalms 112:1

The righteous will live by faith. —Romans 1:17

Who can be better in religion than one who submits his whole self to God, does good—and follows the way of Abraham the true in faith?
—Koran 4:125

Yet faith itself usually comes before obedience, as 2 Corinthians 5:7 reminds us, "We live by faith, not by sight."

Guide me in your truth and teach me, for you are God my Savior.
—Psalms 25:5

And without faith it is impossible to please God, because anyone who comes to Him must believe that He exists, and that He rewards those who earnestly seek Him. —Hebrews 11:6

For believers are those who, when God is mentioned, feel a tremor in their hearts and when they hear his signs rehearsed, find their faith strengthened. —Koran 8:2

And how are we to obey?

Observe my Sabbaths and have reverence for my sanctuary. I am the Lord.
—Leviticus 19:30

Now fear the Lord and serve him with all faithfulness. —Joshua 24:14

We must obey God rather than men. —Acts 5:29

Having faith will bring us an uncommon strength and power.

*Those who hope in the Lord will renew their strength. They will soar
on wings like eagles; they will run and not grow weary, they will walk
and not be faint.* —Isaiah 40:31

*If you have faith as small as a mustard seed, you can say to this mountain,
"Move from here to there," and it will move. Nothing will be impossible
for you.* —Matthew 17:20

*Obey God and His Messenger; and fall into no disputes, lest you lose heart
and your power depart; and be patient and persevering: for God is with those
who patiently persevere.* —Koran 8:46

And obedience brings its own rewards, as well.

If you are willing and obedient, you will eat the best from the land.
—Isaiah 1:19

Well done, good and faithful servant! You have been faithful with a few things;
I will put you in charge of many things. —Matthew 25:21

For believing men and women, for devout men and women, for true men
and women, for men and women who are patient and constant . . .
God has prepared forgiveness and great reward. —Koran 33:35

God is faithful in turn to those who have faith and honor God's ways.

Be careful to obey all the law my servant Moses gave you ... meditate on it day and night, so that you may be careful to do everything written in it. Then you will be prosperous and successful. —Joshua 1:7–8

Then you will have success, if you are careful to observe the decrees and laws that the Lord gave Moses. —1 Chronicles 22:13

Love the Lord, all His saints! The Lord preserves the faithful. —Psalms 31:23

Blessed are those who have not seen and yet have believed. —John 20:29

Everything is possible for him who believes! —Mark 9:23

Be faithful, even to the point of death, and I will give you the crown of life. —Revelation 2:10

The believers must eventually win through—those who are humble themselves in their prayers; who avoid vain talk, who are active in deeds of charity. —Koran 23:1–4

And just what exactly is faith?

I know that my Redeemer lives. —Job 19:25

Faith is being sure of what we hope for and certain of what we do not see.
—Hebrews 11:1

The religion before God is Islam (submission to His will). —Koran 3:19

5. pray

Though each of these three traditions has its own unique methods of prayer—such as the *salat* of Islam, the practice of saying prayers five times a day using physical movement; and the *mitzvah* for Jews to pray three times a day from the Hebrew prayer book called the Siddur—the act of praying is the foundation of the spiritual life in every religion. Prayer is the way we enter into relationship to God; it is our way of communicating with the Mystery.

There are different kinds of prayers; the Jewish distinction between *hodayah* (prayers of thanksgiving), *tehillah* (prayers of praise), and *bakashah* (prayers of request) mirrors the varied Christian prayers of adoration, confession, thanksgiving, and supplication referred to by the acronym ACTS. Sometimes our prayers are said in solitude; sometimes we join with our spiritual community to pray.

No matter what kind of prayer we bring to God, we are encouraged to pray by the holy writings, which tell us not only to be consistent in our practice, but also provide guidelines for our attitude and approach.

But for me, I call to God; and the Lord saves me. Evening, morning, and noon, I cry out in distress, and he hears my voice. —Psalms 55:16–17

Pray continually. —1 Thessalonians 5:17

Enjoin prayer on your people, and be constant therein. —Koran 20:132

~

We are rewarded for coming to God in prayer; we are told that through prayer we will draw close to God, that God will even answer our prayers.

Cast your cares on the Lord and he will sustain you. —Psalms 55:22

The Lord is near to all who call on him, to all who call on him in truth.
—Psalms 145:18

*Whatever you ask for in prayer, believe that you have received it,
and it will be yours.* —Mark 11:24

And our Lord says: "Call on Me; I will answer your prayer."
—Koran 40:60

Yet we need to be mindful of the way in which we enter into prayer; we are instructed that prayer is to come from the heart, and to be done privately, with a sense of reverence.

Do not be quick with your mouth, do not be hasty in your heart to utter anything before God. God is in heaven and you are on earth, so let your words be few. —Ecclesiastes 5:2

But when you pray, go into your room, close the door and pray to your Father, who is unseen. Then your Father, who sees what is done in secret, will reward you. —Matthew 6:8

Neither speak your prayer aloud, nor speak it in a low tone, but seek a middle course between. —Koran 17:110

Call on your Lord with humility and in private. —Koran 7:55

We are told that there is great power in prayer, that through prayer we can access the dynamic forces of God.

He fulfills the desires of those who fear him; he hears their cry and saves them.
—Psalms 145:19

Anyone who has faith in me will do what I have been doing.
He will do even greater things than these, because I am going to the Father.
And I will do whatever you ask in my name, so that the Son may bring
glory to the Father.   —John 14:12–14

Prayer restrains from shameful and unjust deeds; and remembrance of God
is the greatest thing in life, without doubt.   —Koran 29:45

We can trust that God will hear our prayers, because we are told that God loves our prayers.

The Lord detests the sacrifice of the wicked, but the prayer of the upright pleases him. —Proverbs 15:8

Do not be anxious about anything, but in everything, by prayer and petition, with thanksgiving, present your requests to God. —Philippians 4:6

I listen to the prayer of every supplicant when he calls on Me. —Koran 2:186

~

Since we are called in all of the scriptures to love and serve God with all our heart, prayer is our very tangible way of doing so. For as the Talmud (Taan. 2b) reminds us, "which is the service of the heart? Prayer."

6. trust in god

Believing in God, in a God who is Divine Intelligence, implies that we can trust God to do what is best for us. By doing so, we find ourselves changed in the process.

Those who trust in the Lord are like Mount Zion, which cannot be shaken but endures forever. —Psalms 125:1

Blessed is the man who trusts in the Lord, whose confidence is in him. He will be like a tree planted by the water that sends out its roots by the tream. It does not fear when heat comes; its leaves are always green. —Jeremiah 17:7–8

In his great mercy he has given us new birth into a living hope. —1 Peter 1:3

Any who believes in his Lord has no fear, either of a short account or of any injustice. —Koran 72:13

We are told that our trust will not be dishonored; that by trusting God, we will be with God forever.

If I rise on the wings of the dawn, if I settle on the far side of the sea,
even there your hand will guide me, and your right hand will hold me fast.
—Psalms 139:9–10

Neither death nor life, neither angels nor demons, neither the present
nor the future, nor any powers, neither height nor depth, nor anything else
in all creation, will be able to separate us from the love of God.
—Romans 8:38–39

God is the Light of the heavens and the earth. —Koran 24:35

Therefore, no matter what befalls us, we are to maintain our trust in God because our God is a loving God.

Though I walk in the midst of trouble, you preserve my life. —Psalms 138:8

In all things God works for the good of those who love him, who have been called according to His purpose. —Romans 8:28

Be sure we will test you with something of fear and hunger, some loss in goods or lives or the fruits of your toil, but give glad tidings to those who patiently persevere—who say, when afflicted with a calamity: "To God we belong and to Him is our return"—They are those on whom descend blessings from their Lord and mercy, and they are the ones that receive guidance. —Koran 2:155–58

And even when what we see God do defies our senses and our understanding of the ways of the world, God can be trusted no matter what is happening.

Some wandered in desert wastelands, finding no way to a city they could settle. They were hungry and thirsty, and their lives ebbed away. Then they cried out to the Lord in their trouble, and he delivered them from their distress. —Psalms 107:4–6

Without warning, a furious storm came up on the lake, so that the waves swept over the boat. But Jesus was sleeping. The disciples went and woke him, saying, "Lord, save us! We're going to drown!" He replied, "You of little faith, why are you so afraid?" Then he got up and rebuked the winds and the waves, and it was completely calm. —Matthew 8:24–26

[Mary] said, "O my Lord! How shall I have a son when no man has touched me?" He said, "Even so: God creates what He will. When he decrees a plan, He but says to it 'Be,' and it is!" —Koran 3:47

We can trust that whatever is happening is because God wills it to be so for reasons that we may not yet be aware of.

Trust in the Lord with all your heart and lean not on your own understanding;
in all your ways acknowledge Him, and he will make your paths straight.
—Proverbs 3:5–6

Nothing will happen to us except what God has decreed for us.
He is our Protector: and on God let the believers put their trust. —Koran 9:51

By surrendering our ego and placing things in the hands of God, we will find our compensation and comfort.

Be strong and take heart, all you who hope in the Lord. —Psalms 31:24

You will keep in perfect peace him whose mind is steadfast, because he trusts in you. —Isaiah 26:3

And if anyone puts his trust in God, sufficient is God for him. —Koran 65:3

Sometimes trust is even more passive, a simple releasing.

The Lord is good to those whose hope is in him, to the one who seeks him; it is good to wait quietly for the salvation of the Lord. —Lamentations 3:25–26

And why do you worry … ? See how the lilies of the field grow.
They do not labor or spin. Yet I tell you that not even Solomon in all
his splendor was dressed like one of these. —Matthew 6:28–29

And perhaps it all simply comes down to this:

Trust in the Lord, and do good. —Psalms 37:3

7. stay thankful

Members of all faith traditions have been given a wonderful guide-book on how to give thanks in the form of the Book of Psalms. In this section of scripture, the author David shows us that thanks can be given with exuberance and constancy. But even if we are not as poetically inclined as David, we still are to praise God, for God is the source of all our blessings. We give thanks to God because we are gifted by God; all that we receive is due to the beneficence of our Creator.

I will praise your name forever and ever ... and joyfully sing of your righteousness. —Psalms 145:1, 7

Every good and perfect gift is from above. —James 1:17

Your Lord is full of grace to mankind: yet most of them are ungrateful. —Koran 27:73

Everything which He has created [is] most good ... little thanks do you give! —Koran 32:7, 9

God has provided many wonderful things for us; all we are asked to do in return is simply to show gratitude.

Enter his gates with thanksgiving and his courts with praise; give thanks to him and praise his name. For God is good; and his love endures forever; his faithfulness continues through all generations. —Psalms 100:4, 5

And let the peace of God rule in your hearts ... giving thanks to God the Father. —Colossians 3:15, 17

It is He who brought you forth from the wombs of your mothers when you knew nothing; and He gave you hearing and sight and intelligence and affections: that you may give thanks. —Koran 16:78

We are taught how we can show our gratitude.

It is good to praise the Lord, and to make music to Your name, O Most High,
to proclaim Your love in the morning and Your faithfulness at night.
—Psalms 92:1–2

Be joyful always; pray continually; give thanks in all circumstances,
for this is God's will for you. —1 Thessalonians 5:16–18

O you who believe! Eat of the good things that We have provided for you
and be grateful to God, if it is Him you worship. —Koran 2:172

And, as demonstrated in 2 Corinthians 9:15, we do not need to worry about using the "right" words in order to express our thanks: "Thanks be to God for his indescribable gift!"

PART TWO

the principles
concerning others

8. honor your parents

We are all asked to honor our elders and our parents, for reasons in addition to those given in the Talmud (Abodah Zarah, 5a): "Let us ascribe merit to our ancestors; for if they had not sinned we should not have come into the world." We should do so simply because God wishes us to.

Honor your father and your mother, so that you may live long in the land the Lord your God is giving you. —Exodus 20:12

Children, obey your parents in everything, for this pleases the Lord. —Colossians 3:20

We are told that our parents were given very important roles to play, for which they should be honored.

He decreed statutes for Jacob and established the law in Israel, which he commanded our forefathers to teach their children, so the next generation would know them, even the children yet to be born, and they in turn would tell their children. Then they would put their trust in God and would not forget his deeds, but would keep His commands. —Psalms 78:5–7

We have enjoined on man kindness to his parents: In pain did his mother bear him, and in pain did she give him birth. The carrying of the child to his weaning is a period of thirty months. At length, when he reaches the age of full strength and attains forty years, he says, "O my Lord! Grant me that I may be grateful for Your favor which You have bestowed upon me, and upon both my parents, and that I may work righteousness such as You may approve; and be gracious to me in my issue." —Koran 46:15

And we are given instructions as to how we are to honor them.

Listen, my son, to your father's instruction and do not forsake your mother's teaching. —Proverbs 1:8

Children, obey your parents in the Lord: for this is right. —Ephesians 6:1

Your Lord has decreed ... that you be kind to parents. Whether one or both of them attain old age in your life, say not to them a word of contempt, nor repel them, but address them in terms of honor. And, out of kindness, lower to them the wing of humility, and say, "My Lord! Bestow on them Your mercy even as they cherished me in childhood." —Koran 17:23–24

And this solicitation must extend also to the other elders and need-filled in our midst.

Rise in the presence of the aged, show respect for the elderly and revere your God. I am the Lord. —Leviticus 19:32

Do not rebuke an older man harshly, but exhort him as if he were your father. Treat younger men as brothers, older women as mothers, and younger women as sisters, with absolute purity . . . . But if a widow has children or grandchildren, these should learn first of all to put their religion into practice by caring for their own family and so repaying their parents and grandparents, for this is pleasing to God. —1 Timothy 5:1–2, 4

Serve God, and join not any partners with him; and do good—to parents, kinsfolk, orphans, those in need, neighbors who are near, neighbors who are strangers, the companion by your side, the wayfarer you meet, and what your right hands possess. —Koran 4:36

And by doing so, we might just learn something along the way.

Is not wisdom found among the aged? Does not long life bring understanding?
 —Job 12:12

Age should speak; advanced years should teach wisdom. —Job 32:7

9. tell the truth

Telling the truth means that we live in integrity; that all of our behaviors are united and congruent. As the Talmud (Pes. 113b) teaches, "no person should say one thing with his mouth and another in his heart."

Why should we tell the truth? We are told in scripture that it is the very fabric of our relationship to God, and one way that we show our love of God.

Lord, who may dwell in your sanctuary? Who may live on your holy hill? He whose walk is blameless and ... who speaks the truth from his heart.
—Psalms 15:1, 2

God is spirit, and his worshipers must worship in spirit and in truth.
—John 4:24

O you who believe, why say you that which you do not? Grievously odious is it in the sight of God that you say that which you do not.
—Koran 61:2–3

We are told very specifically what matters encompass truth-telling.

You shall not give false testimony against your neighbor. —Exodus 20:16

Do not spread false reports. Do not help a wicked man by being a malicious witness.... Have nothing to do with a false charge. —Exodus 23:1, 7

Do not steal. Do not lie. Do not deceive one another.... Do not go about spreading slander among your people. —Leviticus 19:11, 16

Speak the truth to each other, and render true and sound judgment in your courts. —Zechariah 8:16

And cover not Truth with falsehood, nor conceal the truth when you know what it is. —Koran 2:42

But if anyone earns a fault or a sin and throws it on to one that is innocent, he carries on himself both a falsehood and a flagrant sin. —Koran 4:112

The scriptures teach how important it is to tell the truth; that we risk separation from God if we are deceitful or untruthful.

The Lord detests lying lips, but he delights in men who are truthful.
—Proverbs 12:22

No one who practices deceit will dwell in my house; no one who speaks falsely will stand in my presence. —Psalms 101:7

I tell you that men will have to give account on the day of judgment for every careless word they have spoken. For by your words you will be acquitted, and by your words you will be condemned. —Matthew 12:34–37

But God guides not such as are false and ungrateful. —Koran 39:3

And there are other compelling reasons why we should endeavor to be truthful people.

Truthful lips endure forever, but a lying tongue lasts only a moment.
—Proverbs 12:19

Therefore each of you must put off falsehood and speak truthfully to his neighbor, for we are all members of one body. —Ephesians 4:25

The truth will set you free. —John 8:32

We can all call upon our God to help us in this process.

The Spirit of Truth ... will guide you into all truth. —John 16:13

10. treat others as yourself

Known as the Golden Rule, this principle is the foundation of how we are to conduct our relationships with others. On it, all interactions are grounded.

Do not oppress an alien; you yourselves know how it feels to be aliens, because you were aliens in Egypt. —Exodus 23:9

Love does no harm to its neighbor. Therefore love is the fulfillment of the Law. —Romans 13:10

God commands justice, the doing of good. —Koran 16:90

The message is repeated in our scriptures; we are told in clear, direct words what this principle entails.

Love your neighbor as yourself. —Leviticus 19:18

Do to others what you would have them do to you. —Matthew 7:12

What we are also told is that by demonstrating love to others, we are at the same time demonstrating our love of God.

You are to have the same law for the alien and the native-born.
I am the Lord your God. —Leviticus 24:22

Let us love one another, for love comes from God. Everyone who loves has
been born of God and knows God. Whoever does not love does not know God,
because God is love.... Anyone who does not love his brother, whom he has
seen, cannot love God, whom he has not seen. —1 John 4:7–8, 20

By this all men will know that you are my disciples, if you love one another.
—John 13:35

No reward do I ask of you for this except the love of those near of kin.
—Koran 42:23

And we are given the means to love others, even through that which has caused us great sorrow or been extremely challenging.

Praise be to God, the God of all comfort, who comforts us in all our troubles, so that we can comfort those in any trouble with the comfort we ourselves have received from God. —2 Corinthians 1:3

Our means for treating each other as ourselves are really quite simple.

Live in harmony with one another; be sympathetic, love as brothers,
be compassionate and humble. —1 Peter 3:8

Repel evil with what is better: then will he between whom and you was hatred
become as it were your friend and intimate! —Koran 41:34

And perhaps this line from the Talmud (Shabbat 31a) serves both as a useful summary and an intriguing reflection:

What is hateful to yourself, do not do to your fellow-man.
That is the whole of the Torah, and the remainder is but commentary.

ii. serve and give to others

A natural extension of treating others as ourselves, worshipers in each of these traditions are instructed to be of service to others and to give to those who are poor, hungry, and in need. This is so important that God commands it.

There will always be poor people in the land. Therefore I command you
to be openhanded toward … the poor and needy in your land.
—Deuteronomy 15:11

Religion that God our Father accepts as pure and faultless is this:
to look after the orphans and widows in their distress, and to keep oneself
from being polluted by the world. —James 1:27

So he who gives in charity and fears God, and in all sincerity testifies
to the best—We will indeed make smooth for him the path to Bliss.
But he who is a greedy miser and thinks himself self-sufficient …
we will indeed make smooth for him the path to Misery. —Koran 92:5–10

We are told that living this principle has ramifications for our very soul.

A kind man benefits himself. —Proverbs 11:17

Be merciful just as your Father is merciful. . . . Give, and it will be given to you. A good measure, pressed down, shaken together, and running over, will be poured into your lap. For with the measure you use, it will be measured to you. —Luke 6:36, 38

Behold, you are those invited to spend of your substance in the way of God: but among you are some that are miserly. But any who are miserly are so at the expense of their own souls. —Koran 47:38

Our gifts are not to be given grudgingly; they are to be offered with an open heart.

Worship the Lord with gladness. —Psalms 100:2

Not reluctantly or under compulsion, for God loves a cheerful giver. —2 Corinthians 9:7

Freely you have received, freely give. —Matthew 10:8

O you who believe! Cancel not your charity by reminders of your generosity or by injury. —Koran 2:264

And we are not to make great show of our service to others; preferably, it will be done quietly and even anonymously.

But when you give to the needy, do not let your left hand know what your right hand is doing, so that your giving may be in secret. —Matthew 6:3–4

If you disclose acts of charity, even so it is well, but if you conceal them, and make them reach those really in need, that is best for you. —Koran 2:271

We are rewarded by God for serving those who cross our path.

Blessed is he who has regard for the weak; the Lord delivers him in times of trouble. —Psalms 41:1

He who gives to the poor will lack nothing. —Proverbs 28:27

Blessed are the merciful, for they will be shown mercy. —Matthew 5:7

And, of a surety, to all will your Lord pay back in full the recompense of their deeds: for He knows well all that they do. —Koran 11:111

Yet we should give to others out of our love for God, not because we expect to be or want to be rewarded.

I the Lord search the heart and examine the mind, to reward a man according to his conduct, according to what his deeds deserve. —Jeremiah 17:10

This service that you perform is not only supplying the needs of God's people but is also overflowing in many expressions of thanks to God. —2 Corinthians 9:12

And they feed, for the love of God, the indigent, the orphan, and the captive— saying, "We feed you for the sake of God alone: No reward do we desire from you, nor thanks." —Koran 76:8–9

Doing good for others, giving to them in service, is simply a hall-mark of a faithful human being. We do good for good's sake; because, simply, it is the right and responsible thing to do. This is understood well in Judaism; the Hebrew word *tzedukah*, translated as "charity," comes from a root word meaning "justice" or "righteousness."

The righteous give generously. —Psalms 37:21

If anyone has material possessions and sees his brother in need but has no pity on him, how can the love of God be in Him? Dear children, let us not love with words or tongue; but with actions and in truth. —1 John 3:17–18

Therefore, as we have opportunity, let us do good to all people.
—Galatians 6:10

On those who believe and do deeds of righteousness there is no blame ... for God loves those who do good. —Koran 5:93

And lest we think that we are exempt from giving if we ourselves have little money, the Talmud (Git. 7b) teaches that "Even the beggar who is maintained by charity must himself practice charity." Similarly, the Hadith instructs that charity is a duty of every Muslim, that the person who has no money can "do good deeds and refrain from doing evil—this is charity on his part" (B. 24:30). Given this, we are shown many ways to give in the scriptures.

Learn to do right! Seek justice, encourage the oppressed. Defend the cause of the fatherless, plead for the case of the widow. —Isaiah 1:17

Do not withhold good from those who deserve it, when it is in your power to act. —Proverbs 3:27

Share with God's people who are in need. Practice hospitality. —Romans 12:13

Command them to do good, to be rich in good deeds, and to be generous and willing to share. —1 Timothy 6:18

Offer hospitality to one another without grumbling. —1 Peter 4:9

The man with two tunics should share with him who has none, and the one who has food should do the same. —Luke 3:11

And the Hadith is even more explicit about things that we can do for others that constitute service to them.

On every bone of the fingers charity is incumbent everyday: One assists
a man in riding a beast or in lifting his provisions to the back of an animal,
this is charity; and a good word and every step which one takes in walking
over to prayer is charity; and showing the way to another is charity.
—Hadith (B. 56:72)

Given the importance of this principle in all three traditions, it seems that all worshipers of God would agree that

As the body without the spirit is dead, so faith without deeds is dead.
—James 2:26

12. don't study the faults of others

Though the scriptures of Christianity are very explicit about not judging others, this principle is also found in the holy writings of Judaism and Islam—most usually, in the Talmud and the Hadith. In all traditions, we learn that we are not to look at the faults of others lest we overlook our own.

Be the cursed and not the curser. —Talmud (Sanh. 49a)

Why do you notice the splinter in your brother's eye, but do not perceive the wooden beam in your own: How can you say to your brother, "Brother, let me remove that splinter in your eye" when you do not even notice the wooden beam in your own eye? You hypocrite! Remove the wooden beam from your eye first; then you will see clearly to remove the splinter in your brother's eye. —Luke 6:41–42

A man does not accuse another of being a transgresso ... but it (the epithet) comes back to him. —Hadith (B. 78:44)

God is the ultimate judge, not us—and should we take that job upon ourselves, we risk having that behavior judged.

Let your fellow-man's honor be as dear to you as your own.
—Talmud (Aboth II, 15)

Do not complain, brethren, against one another, that you yourselves may not be judged; behold, the Judge is standing right at the door. —James 5:9

He who obeys the Messenger, obeys God; but if any turn away, We have not sent you to watch over their evil deeds. —Koran 4:80

We learn that we are not to speak about others in negative terms, that part of the conduct of the faithful is to turn from such behaviors—and that doing this is what God asks of us.

Because you judged me charitably, may God also judge you charitably.
—Talmud (Shabbat 127b)

Do not judge, or you too will be judged. For in the same way you judge others, you will be judged, and with the measure you use, it will be measured to you.
—Matthew 7:1, 2

O you who believe! Let not some men among you laugh at others:
It may be that the latter are better than the former.... Nor defame nor be
sarcastic to each other, nor call each other by offensive nicknames ...
and those who do not desist are indeed doing wrong. —Koran 49:11

For God has standards of which we aren't always—nor can we ever be—aware.

But the Lord said to Samuel, Do not consider his appearance or his height, for I have rejected him. The Lord does not look at the things man looks at. Man looks on the outward appearance, but the Lord looks at the heart.
—1 Samuel 16:7

The man who eats everything must not look down on him who does not, and the man who does not eat everything must not condemn the man who does, for God has accepted him. —Romans 14:3

Your goal in the end is towards God: He will tell you the truth of the things wherein you disputed. —Koran 6:164

Therefore we are well counseled, as Romans 14:13 encourages us, to

Stop passing judgment on one another. Instead, make up your mind not to put any stumbling block or obstacle in your brother's way.

13. forgive

Forgiveness is a principle that we are called to exercise repeatedly in our lives—and for as many times as it takes.

"Lord, how many times shall I forgive my brother when he sins against me?
Up to seven times?" Jesus answered, "I tell you, not seven times,
but seventy-seven times." —Matthew 18:21–22

We are to model the compassion that we wish God to have on us, loving forgiveness of our transgressions.

I, even I, am he that blots out your transgressions, for my own sake, and remembers your sins no more. —Isaiah 43:25

Be merciful, just as your Father is merciful. —Luke 6:36

For if you forgive men when they sin against you, your heavenly Father will also forgive you. —Matthew 6:14

Bear with each other and forgive whatever grievances you may have against one another. Forgive as the Lord forgave you. —Colossians 3:13

If you forgive and overlook, and cover up their faults, truly God is oft-forgiving, most merciful. —Koran 64:14

We will be rewarded by God for our forgiveness.

Blessed is he whose transgressions are forgiven, whose sins are covered.
—Psalms 32:1

If a person forgives and makes reconciliation, his reward is due from God.
—Koran 42:40

~

And by doing this we are able to demonstrate how God is work-ing in our lives.

A man's wisdom gives him patience; it is to his glory to overlook an offense.
—Proverbs 19:11

Be kind and compassionate to one another, forgiving each other, just as ...
God forgave you. —Ephesians 4:32

That which is with God is better and more lasting: It is for those
who believe and put their trust in their Lord; those who ...
when they are angry, even then forgive. —Koran 42:36–37

Forgiveness also includes these characteristics:

Do not gloat when your enemy falls; when he stumbles, do not let your heart rejoice. —Proverbs 24:17

First go and be reconciled to your brother, then come and offer your gift. —Matthew 5:24

Hold to forgiveness, command what is right; but turn away from the ignorant. If a suggestion from Satan assails your mind, seek refuge with God; for he hears and knows all things. —Koran 7:199–200

Kind words and covering of faults are better than charity followed by injury. —Koran 2:263

And not forgiving has its own list of characteristics to be avoided and pitfalls to be risked.

Do not be quickly provoked in your spirit, for anger resides in the lap of fools.
—Ecclesiastes 7:9

In your anger do not sin: Do not let the sun go down while you are still angry, and do not give the devil a foothold. —Ephesians 4:26–27

And lest we think we can shelve it for a later day, 2 Corinthians 2:7
tells us that

Now instead, you ought to forgive and comfort him,
so that he will not be overwhelmed by excessive sorrow.

14. be kind to all creatures

In the scriptures of all three traditions, we are taught that our kindness is not only to extend to our fellow human beings, but also to the animals with which we share the earth. They, too, are the creations of God, and as such we are to care for them with the same kindness with which we are treated by God.

*Your love, O Lord, reaches to the heavens; your faithfulness reaches
to the skies. Your righteousness is like the mighty mountains, your justice
like the great deep. O Lord, you preserve both man and beast. How priceless
is your unfailing love!* —Psalms 36:5, 7

*And God has created every animal from water: Of them there are some
that creep on their bellies; some that walk on two legs; and some that walk
on four. God creates what He wills; for truly God has power over all things.*
—Koran 24:45

Analogies are often used in the scriptures to equate our relationships with animals to God's relationship to us. Through God's provision to animals, we can trust that we too will be provided for.

Suppose one of you has a hundred sheep and loses one of them. Does he not leave the ninety-nine in the open country, and go after the lost sheep until he finds it? —Luke 15:4

Are not five sparrows sold for two pennies? Yet not one of them is forgotten by God.... Consider the ravens: They do not sow or reap, they have no storeroom or barn, yet God feeds them. —Luke 12:6, 24

Look at the birds of the air; they do not sow or reap or store away in barns; and yet your heavenly Father feeds them. —Matthew 6:26

How many are the creatures that carry not their own sustenance? It is God who feeds both them and you. —Koran 29:60

We are told explicitly in the Talmud and Hadith that we are to prevent pain to an animal, that we are to be kind to animals.

A prostitute was forgiven—she passed by a dog, panting with its tongue out, on the top of a well containing water, almost dying of thirst; so she took off her boot and tied it to her head-covering and drew forth water for it; she was forgiven on account of this. It was said: "Is there a reward for us in doing good to the beasts?" He said: "In every animal having a liver fresh with life there is a reward." —Hadith (B. and M-Msh. 6:6)

And we are also told indirectly, through stories, how we are to care for other creatures.

For six years you are to sow your fields and harvest the crops; but during the seventh year let the land lie unplowed and unused. Then the poor among your people may get food from it; and the wild animals may eat what they leave. Do the same with your vineyard and your olive grove. —Exodus 23:10–11

This is what the Sovereign Lord says: Woe to the shepherds of Israel who only take care of themselves! Should not shepherds take care of the flock? You eat the curds, clothe yourselves with the wool and slaughter the choice animals, but you do not take care of the flock. You have not strengthened the weak or healed the sick or bound up the injured. You have not brought back the strays or searched for the lost. You have ruled them harshly and brutally. —Ezekiel 34:2–4

We can learn from the creatures around us.

But ask the animals, and they will teach you, or the birds of the air, and they will tell you; or speak to the earth, and it will teach you, or let the fish of the sea inform you. —Job 12:7

~

And we are to know that God has a special place for them too.

The earth is the Lord's, and everything in it, the world, and all who live in it. —Psalms 24:1

How many are your works, O Lord! In wisdom you made them all; the earth is full of your creatures. —Psalms 104:24

There is no moving creature on earth but its sustenance depends on God: He knows the time and place of its definite abode and its temporary deposit. —Koran 11:6

My mercy extends to all things. —Koran 7:156

There is not an animal that lives on the earth, nor a being that flies on its wings, but forms part of communities like you. Nothing have We omitted from the Book, and they all will be gathered to their Lord in the end. —Koran 6:38

We are to respect the importance of life.

Anyone who is among the living has hope—even a live dog is better off than a dead lion. —Ecclesiastes 9:4

~

For we have been given a special trust.

You made him ruler over the works of your hands; you put everything under his feet: all flocks and herds, all the beasts of the field, the birds of the air, and the fish of the sea, all that swim in the paths of the seas. —Psalms 8:6–8

the principles
concerning self

15. cultivate wisdom

The scriptures of all three traditions have much to say about wisdom; indeed, it is seen as one of the most valuable hallmarks of human life—"more precious than rubies," as Proverbs 8:11 teaches us (and perhaps there is no better book for studying wisdom than the Book of Proverbs). For Muslims, knowledge is deeply important; indeed, the Hadith teaches that "The seeking of knowledge is obligatory" (Bhq-Msh. 2).

The basic foundation for wisdom in all traditions is belief in God.

The fool says in his heart, "There is no God." —Psalms 14:1

The fear of the Lord is the beginning of wisdom; and knowledge of the Holy One is understanding. —Proverbs 9:10

We also learn what other attributes characterize wisdom.

He who walks with the wise grows wise. —Proverbs 13:20

Wisdom brightens a man's face and changes its hard appearance.
—Ecclesiastes 8:1

A man of knowledge uses words with restraint, and a man of understanding is even-tempered. —Proverbs 17:27

For the Lord gives wisdom, and from his mouth comes knowledge and understanding.... Wisdom will enter your heart, and knowledge will be pleasant to your soul. Discretion will protect you, and understanding will guard you. —Proverbs 2:6, 10–11

Whatever is true, whatever is noble, whatever is right, whatever is pure, whatever is lovely, whatever is admirable—if any thing is excellent or praiseworthy—think about such things. —Philippians 4:8

Be as shrewd as snakes, and as innocent as doves. —Matthew 10:16

We also learn what wisdom is not.

Do not be wise in your own eyes. —Proverbs 3:7

Let not the wise man boast of his wisdom. —Jeremiah 9:23

A man who lacks judgment derides his neighbors,
but a man of understanding holds his tongue. —Proverbs 11:12

Reckless words pierce like a sword,
but the tongue of the wise brings healing. —Proverbs 12:18

There are many rewards for attaining wisdom.

A wise man has great power,
and a man of knowledge increases strength. —Proverbs 24:5

Eat honey, my son, for it is good; honey from the comb is sweet to your taste.
Know also that wisdom is sweet to your soul; if you find it, there is a future
for you, and your hope will not be cut off. —Proverbs 24:13–14

The learned ones are the heirs of the prophets—they leave knowledge as their
inheritance; he who inherits it inherits a great fortune. —Hadith (B. 3:10)

Above all we are to acknowledge that wisdom is a gift from God and an understanding of God.

Surely you desire truth in the inner parts, you teach me wisdom in the inmost place. —Psalms 51:6

The wisdom that comes from heaven is first of all pure, then peace-loving, considerate, submissive, full of mercy and good fruit, impartial and sincere. —James 3:17

God … may give you the Spirit of wisdom and revelation, so that you may know him better. —Ephesians 1:17–19

And if we are truly wise, we will let God direct our paths.

In his heart a man plans his course, but the Lord determines his steps.
—Proverbs 16:9

Asking God to fill you with the knowledge of his will through all spiritual wisdom and understanding. —Colossians 1:9

Therefore everyone who hears these words of mine and puts them into practice is like a wise man who built his house on the rock. —Matthew 7:24

He who goes forth in search of knowledge is in the [path] of God.
—Hadith (Tr. 39:2)

Those who listen to the Word, and follow the best meaning in it:
Those are the ones whom God has guided, and those are the ones endued with understanding. —Koran 39:18

True wisdom is distinguished in these ways.

By wisdom a house is built, and through understanding it is established;
through knowledge its rooms are filled with rare and beautiful treasures.
—Proverbs 24:3–4

The wisdom of this world is foolishness in God's sight. —1 Corinthians 3:19

Knowledge puffs up, but love builds up. The man who thinks he knows
something does not yet know as he ought to know. But the man who loves
God is known by God. —1 Corinthians 8:1–3

And God is pleased that we desire wisdom, as this story illustrates.

"So give your servant a discerning heart to govern your people and to distinguish between right and wrong. For who is able to govern this great people of yours?" The Lord was pleased that Solomon had asked for this. So God said to him, "Since you have asked for this and not for long life or wealth for yourself, nor have asked for the death of your enemies ... I will give you a wise and discerning heart; so that there will never have been anyone like you, nor will there ever be." —1 Kings 3:9–12

16. practice self-control

For the faithful, the difference between a life that's godly and one that's not can hinge on the practice of self-control. This lies at the heart of the struggle for most human beings; even Paul in the Christian scriptures and Muhammad in the Hadith acknowledge the difficulty of the struggle with the lower self. Self-control begins with the commandments, with acts that we know to be wrong.

You shall not murder. You shall not commit adultery. You shall not steal.
You shall not give false testimony against your neighbor. You shall not
covet your neighbor's house. You shall not covet your neighbor's wife,
or his manservant or maidservant, his ox, his donkey, or anything that
belongs to your neighbor. —Exodus 20:13–17

It includes self-control of the body.

Offer your bodies as living sacrifices, holy and pleasing to God.
—Romans 12:1

Abstain from sinful desires, which war against your soul. —1 Peter 2:11

Eat and drink: but waste not by excess, for God loves not the wasters.
—Koran 7:31

~

Self-control also encompasses one's mind and emotional responses.

*Better a patient man than a warrior, a man who controls his temper
than one who takes a city.* —Proverbs 16:32

And I strive always to keep my conscience clear before God and men.
—Acts 24:16

Do everything without complaining or arguing. —Philippians 2:14

You have heard that it was said to the people long ago, "Do not murder, and anyone who murders will be subject to judgment." But I tell you that anyone who is angry with his brother will be subject to judgment.
—Matthew 5:21–22

What causes fights and quarrels among you? Don't they come from your desires that battle within you? You want something but don't get it. You kill and covet, but you cannot have what you want. You quarrel and fight. You do not have, because you do not ask God. When you ask, you do not receive, because you ask with wrong motives, that you may spend what you get on your pleasures. —James 4:1–3

Do not hate one another and do not be jealous of one another and do not boycott one another....and it is not lawful for a Muslim that he should sever his relations with his brother for more than three days. —Hadith (B. 78:57)

Be courteous, and keep thyself away from roughness. —Hadith (B. 78:38)

We will be helped by God in our quest to overcome temptation.

"The evil one watches the righteous and seeks to slay him" (Ps. 37:32). *And were it not for the fact that the Holy One ... is his support, he would be unable to withstand it.* —Talmud (Kiddushin 30b)

No temptation has seized you except what is common to man;
God is faithful; he will not let you be tempted beyond what you can bear.
But when you are tempted, he will also provide a way out so that you
can stand up under it. —1 Corinthians 10:12–13

My grace is sufficient for you, for my power is made perfect in weakness.
—2 Corinthians 12:9

Finally, be strong in the Lord and in his mighty power.
Put on the full armor of God. —Ephesians 6:10

On no soul does God place a burden greater than it can bear. —Koran 2:286

We practice self-control as a mark of the faithful, as a way to move past that which has kept us from God so that we might be more fully in God's presence.

The wicked are under control of their heart, but the righteous have their heart under their control. —Talmud (Gen. R. 34:10)

Let us throw off everything that hinders, and the sin that so easily entangles, and let us run with perseverance the race marked out for us. —Hebrews 12:1–2

Flee the evil desires of youth, and pursue righteousness, faith, love and peace, along with those who call on the Lord out of a pure heart. —2 Timothy 2:22

Blessed is the man who perseveres under trial because when he has stood the test, he will win the crown of life that God has promised to those who love him. —James 1:12

But such as comes to Him as believers, who have worked righteous deeds ... Gardens of Eternity, beneath which flow rivers; they will dwell therein forever. Such is the reward of those who purify themselves from evil. —Koran 20:75–76

And we will be helped if we see God as being indwelling, living in our own bodies.

A person should always consider that there is a holy component to his physical self. —Talmud (Taanit 11a–11b)

Your body is a temple of the Holy Spirit, who is in you, whom you have received from God. You are not your own. —1 Corinthians 6:19

We are to be vigilant about becoming too lax.

As a dog returns to its vomit, so a fool repeats his folly. —Proverbs 26:11

Watch and pray so that you will not fall into temptation.
The spirit is willing, but the body is weak. —Matthew 26:41

Be self-controlled and alert. —1 Peter 5:8

Nor can Goodness and Evil be equal. Repel evil with what is better.
—Koran 41:34

For earthly pleasures pale in comparison with spiritual understanding.

The Spirit gives life; the flesh counts for nothing. —John 6:63

Those who seek gain in evil, and are girt round by their sins—they are companions of the fire: Therein shall they abide forever. —Koran 2:81

~

The ultimate prescription for self-control?

So whether you eat or drink or whatever you do,
do it all for the glory of God. —1 Corinthians 10:31

17. develop your character

Though the *surahs*, or passages, of the Koran are currently arranged from longest to shortest, there have been many who have attempted to ascertain in which order the *surahs* of the Koran were given to Muhammad. The following, which seems an appropriate introduction to the subject of developing one's character, is considered to very possibly have been the first one Muhammad received.

And your Lord do you glorify and your garments keep free from stain!
And all abomination shun! —Koran 74:3–5

The flip side of practicing self-control, developing one's character has a more active, even creative, component: that of building or moving toward something, as opposed to simply restraining oneself or escaping something. By doing so, we move toward God, emulating to the best of our abilities the nature of God.

I am God Almighty; walk before me and be blameless. —Genesis 17:1

Be perfect therefore, as your heavenly father is perfect. —Matthew 5:48

~

Our righteousness is something God desires.

Teach me your way, O Lord, and I will walk in your truth. —Psalms 86:11

Equip you with everything good for doing his will, and may he work in us what is pleasing to him. —Hebrews 13:21

But God has endeared the faith to you, and has made it beautiful in your hearts, and he has made hateful to you unbelief, wickedness, and rebellion: such indeed are those who walk in righteousness. —Koran 49:7

And we do not need to guess just how we are to develop our character; we are told in the scriptures what that constitutes.

Let love and faithfulness never leave you: bind them around your neck, write them on the tablet of your heart. —Proverbs 3:3

Live as children of light (for the fruit of the light consists in all goodness, righteousness and truth). —Ephesians 5:8–9

Set an example for the believers in speech, in life, in love, in faith, and in purity. —1 Timothy 4:12

Flee the evil desires of youth and pursue righteousness, faith, love and peace, along with those who call on the Lord out of a pure heart. —2 Timothy 2:21–22

The fruit of the Spirit is love, joy, peace, patience, kindness, goodness, faithfulness, gentleness, and self-control. —Galatians 5:22

God commands justice, the doing of good, and liberality to kith and kin; and He forbids all shameful deeds, and injustice, and rebellion. —Koran 16:90

We will be blessed for our efforts to do this work.

He who pursues righteousness and love finds life, prosperity, and honor.
—Proverbs 21:21

The righteous will flourish like a palm tree; they will grow like a cedar of Lebanon. —Psalms 92:12

The righteous cannot be uprooted. —Proverbs 12:3

The man who looks intently into the perfect law that gives freedom, and continues to do this, not forgetting what he has heard, but doing it— he will be blessed in whatever he does. —James 1:25

Truly the righteous will be in bliss. —Koran 83:22

The most honored of you in the sight of God is he who is the most righteous of you. —Koran 49:13

And if we don't do this work of developing our characters, we will be lost.

Above all else, guard your heart, for it is the wellspring of life.
—Proverbs 4:23

Can a blind man lead a blind man? Will they not both fall into a pit?
A student is not above his teacher: but everyone who is fully trained will be
like his teacher. —Luke 6:39–40

By the token of time through the ages, truly man is in loss, except such as
have faith, and do righteous deeds, and join together in the mutual teaching
of truth, and of patience and constancy. —Koran 103:1–3

We must be consistent and steadfast in our attempts to live a life of character.

Create in me a pure heart, O God, and renew a steadfast spirit within me.
—Psalms 51:10

Never tire of doing what is right. —2 Thessalonians 3:13

But if we give him a taste of our favors after adversity has touched him, he is sure to say "All evil has departed from me"; Behold! He falls into exultation and pride. Not so do those who show patience and constancy, and work righteousness; for them is forgiveness of sins and a great reward.
—Koran 11:10–12

And we do this to show that God is with and within us.

Oh, praise the greatness of our God! He is the Rock, his works are perfect.
—Deuteronomy 32:3–4

I urge you to live a life worthy of the calling you have received.
—Ephesians 4:1

But whoever lives by the truth comes into the light, so that it may be seen plainly that what he has done has been done through God. —John 3:21

Let your light shine before men, that they all may see your good deeds and praise your Father in heaven. —Matthew 5:16

There is a mosque whose foundation was laid from the first day on piety; it is more worthy for you to stand in. In it are men who love to be purified; and God loves those who make themselves pure. —Koran 9:108

God will help us in our efforts.

He guides me in paths of righteousness for his name's sake. —Psalms 23:3

I have set you an example that you should do as I have done for you.
—John 13:15

Blessed are those who hunger and thirst for righteousness, for they will be filled.
—Matthew 5:6

O you who believe! Do your duty to God, seek the means of approach
unto Him, and strive with might and main in His cause: that you prosper.
—Koran 5:35

But developing our characters will not happen without the will and
the work of each individual believer.

Let us discern for ourselves what is right; let us learn together what is good.
—Job 34:4

This is my prayer ... that you may be able to discern what is best
and may be pure and blameless ... filled with the fruit of righteousness.
—Philippians 1:9–11

O you who believe! Guard your own souls ... never will God change
the condition of a people until they change it themselves with their own souls.
—Koran 5:105 and 13:11

And the act of developing our characters might be its own reward, as this question suggests.

Is there any Reward for Good—other than Good? —Koran 55:60

18. remain humble

Humility is an important virtue for believers in these faith traditions; for while we are children of God, we are not God. Therefore we are counseled to keep our spirit humble, to remember our place in the larger perspective.

The fear of the Lord teaches a man wisdom; and humility comes before honor.
—Proverbs 15:33

Let the little children come to me, and do not hinder them, for the kingdom of God belongs to such as these. I tell you the truth, anyone who will not receive the kingdom of God like a little child will never enter it. —Mark 10:14

Who is it that delivers you from the dark recesses of land and sea; when you call upon Him in humility and in silent terror: "If He only delivers us from these dangers we vow we shall surely show our gratitude"? Say: "It is God that delivers you from these and all other distresses." —Koran 6:64

By being humble, we will be rewarded, for this is how we honor God.

Great is our Lord and mighty in power; His understanding has no limit.
The Lord sustains the humble, but casts the wicked to the ground.
—Psalms 147:5–6

All of you, clothe yourselves with humility toward one another....
Humble yourselves, therefore, under God's mighty hand, that he may lift
you up in due time. —1 Peter 5:5–6

For men and women who humble themselves ... and women who are humble
... God prepared forgiveness and great reward. —Koran 33:35

Therein lies the great paradox: that by being humble, we are to be exalted.

But the meek will inherit the land and enjoy great peace. —Psalms 37:11

Humility and the fear of the Lord bring wealth and honor and life.
—Proverbs 22:4

Whoever will become great among you must be your servant,
and who wants to be first must be your slave. —Matthew 20:26–27

He who is least among you all—he is the greatest. —Luke 9:48

Seek God's help with patient perseverance and prayer: it is indeed hard,
except to those who bring a lowly spirit—who bear in mind the certainty
that they are to meet their Lord, and that they are to return to Him.
—Koran 2:45–46

Conversely, by not being humble, we risk God's wrath.

Should you then seek great things for yourself? Seek them not.
—Jeremiah 45:5

A man's pride brings him low; but a man of lowly spirit gains honor.
—Proverbs 29:23

*Better to be lowly in spirit and among the oppressed than to share plunder
with the proud.* —Proverbs 16:19

*Whoever exalts himself will be humbled, and whoever humbles himself
will be exalted.* —Matthew 23:12

God opposes the proud but gives grace to the humble. —James 4:6

*Do nothing out of selfish ambition or vain conceit, but in humility
consider others better than yourselves.* —Philippians 2:3

*And swell not your cheek for pride at men in scorn, nor walk in insolence
through the earth: for God does not love any arrogant boaster.
And be moderate in your pace and lower your voice; for the harshest
of all sounds without doubt is the braying of the ass.* —Koran 31:18–19

There are specific characteristics that define humility.

*What does the Lord require of you? To act justly and to love mercy
and to walk humbly with your God.* —Micah 6:8

*Your inner self, the unfading beauty of a gentle and quiet spirit,
which is of great worth in God's sight.... Finally, all of you, live in harmony
with one another; be sympathetic, love as brothers, be compassionate and
humble.* —1 Peter 3:4, 8

*Therefore ... clothe yourselves with compassion, kindness, humility,
gentleness, and patience.* —Colossians 3:12

*The believers must eventually win through those who humble themselves
in their prayers; who avoid vain talk; who are active in deeds of charity.*
—Koran 23:1–4

Looking to God is how we are to become humble; God will show us the way.

He guides the humble in what is right and teaches them his way.
—Psalms 25:9

Jesus said to his disciples, "If anyone would come after me, he must deny himself and take up his cross and follow me." —Matthew 16:24

Give the good news to those who humble themselves—to those whose hearts, when God is mentioned, are filled with fear. —Koran 22:34–35

And, should any person be tempted to boast, there is an antidote.

My soul will boast in the Lord. —Psalms 34:2

Let him who boasts boast in the Lord. —2 Corinthians 10:17

19. admit your mistakes

In our life with God, repentance can take two forms: being sorrowful for our mistakes, and being sorrowful for not having believed.

We are expressly asked by God to admit our mistakes.

When a man or woman wrongs another in any way and so is unfaithful
to the Lord, that person is guilty and must confess the sin he has committed.
—Numbers 5:5–7

Repent, for the kingdom of heaven is near. —Matthew 3:2

And ask forgiveness for your fault, and celebrate the praises of your Lord
in the evening and in the morning. —Koran 40:55

God shows great joy and forgiveness when we acknowledge our errors.

As surely as I live, declares the Sovereign Lord, I take no pleasure in the death of the wicked, but rather that they turn from their ways and live. Turn, turn from your evil ways! —Ezekiel 33:11

There will be more rejoicing in heaven over one sinner who repents, than over ninety-nine righteous persons who do not need to repent. —Luke 15:7

God loves those who turn to Him constantly, and He loves those who keep themselves pure and clean. —Koran 2:222

All God requires is a sorrowful and contrite heart.

I live in a high and holy place, but also with him who is contrite and lowly in spirit, to revive the spirit of the lowly, and to revive the heart of the contrite. —Isaiah 57:15

The sacrifices of God are a broken spirit; a broken and contrite heart, O God, you will not despise. —Psalms 51:17

Godly sorrow brings repentance that leads to salvation. —2 Corinthians 7:10

Ask forgiveness of your Lord, and turn towards him in repentance: for my Lord is indeed full of mercy and loving-kindness. —Koran 11:90

We are not only taught to admit our mistakes, but even given words for how to do so.

How many wrongs and sins have I committed?
Show me my offenses and my sin. —Job 13:23

Wash away all my iniquity and cleanse me from my sin ... Against you,
you only, have I sinned, and done what is evil in your sight. —Psalms 51:2, 4

Then Saul said, "I have sinned ... surely I have acted like a fool
and have erred greatly." —1 Samuel 26:21

Forgive us our sins. —Luke 11:4

For in God's sight are all His servants—namely those who say:
"Our Lord! We have indeed believed: forgive us, then, our sins, and save us."
—Koran 3:15–16

There is great power in admitting our mistakes, for our mistakes will be forgiven.

Though your sins are like scarlet, they shall be as white as snow.
—Isaiah 1:18

If we confess our sins, he is faithful and just and will forgive us our sins and purify us from all unrighteousness. —1 John 1:9

He repents, believes and works righteous deeds; for God will change the evil of such persons into good, and God is oft-Forgiving, Most Merciful.
—Koran 25:70

No one is exempt from making mistakes.

There is not a righteous man on earth, who does what is right and never sins.
—Ecclesiastes 7:20

If we claim to be without sin, we deceive ourselves. —1 John 1:8

If any one of you is without sin, let him be the first to throw a stone.
—John 8:7

Every soul will be held in pledge for its deeds. —Koran 74:38

~

But we are not to be careless with our gift of forgiveness; ultimately
we can show our true repentance in this way.

Produce fruits in keeping with repentance. —Luke 3:8

20. be a peacemaker

It is peace that our hearts desire, and peace which God desires for us. Ultimately, the sum of all the principles add up to the creation of peace—in our own lives, in our communities, in our world.

In our own lives, we are guided as to what will create peace.

Submit to God, and be at peace with him; in this way prosperity will come to you. —Job 22:21

You are near, O Lord, and all your commands are true....
Great peace have they who love your law. —Psalms 119:151, 165

The peace of God, which transcends all understanding. —Philippians 4:7

In the remembrance of God do hearts find satisfaction. —Koran 13:28

In our larger communities, we are also guided as to what will create peace.

Turn from evil and do good; seek peace, and pursue it. —Psalms 34:14

If it is possible, as far as it depends on you, live at peace with everyone.
—Romans 12:18

Let us therefore make every effort to do what leads to peace and to mutual edification. —Romans 14:19

Love your enemies and pray for those who persecute you. —Matthew 5:44

The servants of God Most Gracious are those who walk on the earth in humility, and when the ignorant address them, they say: "Peace!"
—Koran 25:63

And hold fast, all together, by the Rope which God stretched out for you, and be not divided among yourselves; and remember with gratitude God's favor on you; for you were enemies and he joined your hearts in love, so that by His grace, you became brothers. —Koran 3:103

We can ask God for help in creating peace.

Glory to God in the highest, and on earth peace. —Luke 2:14

Say: Praise be to God, and peace on His servants. —Koran 27:59

And we know that we will please God by working for peace.

How beautiful on the mountains are the feet of those who bring good news, who proclaim peace. —Isaiah 52:7

Peacemakers who sow in peace raise a harvest of righteousness. —James 3:18

Make every effort to keep the unity of the Spirit through the bond of peace. —Ephesians 4:3

Blessed are the peacemakers, for they shall be called the sons of God. —Matthew 5:9

The recompense for an injury is an injury equal in degree, but if a person forgives and makes reconciliation, his reward is due from God: for God does not love those who do wrong. —Koran 42:40

Finally, returning to the oldest scriptures, we children of Abraham find great reason to share our hope for peace.

The Lord blesses his people with peace. —Psalms 29:11

They will beat their swords into plowshares, and their spears into pruning hooks: nation shall not take up sword against nation, nor will they train for war any more. —Isaiah 2:4

The wolf will live with the lamb,
The leopard will lie down with the goat;
The calf and the lion and the yearling together;
And a little child will lead them.
The cow will feed with the bear;
Their young will lie down together;
And the lion will eat straw like the ox.
The infant will play near the hole of the cobra;
And the young child put his hand into the viper's nest.
They will neither harm nor destroy on all my holy mountain;
For the earth will be full of the knowledge of the Lord,
As the waters cover the sea. —Isaiah 11

resources for further study

books

Ali, Abdullah Yusuf. *The Meaning of the Holy Qur'an.* Beltsville, MD: Amana Publications, 2001.

Ali, Maulana Muhammad. *A Manual of Hadith.* Columbus, OH: The Ahmadiyya Anjuman Ishaat Islam Lahore Inc., 2001.

Ariel, David S. *What Do Jews Believe? The Spiritual Foundations of Judaism.* New York: Schocken Books, 1995.

Armstrong, Karen. *A History of God: The 4,000-Year Quest of Judaism, Christianity, and Islam.* New York: Ballantine Books, 1994.

———. *Jerusalem: One City, Three Faiths.* New York: Alfred A. Knopf, 1996.

Barnstone, Willis, ed. *The Other Bible: Jewish Pseudepigrapha, Christian Apocrypha, Gnostic Scriptures, Kabbalah, Dead Sea Scrolls.* New York: HarperSanFrancisco, 1984.

Bokser, Ben Zion, trans. *The Talmud: Selected Writings.* Mahwah, NJ: Paulist Press, 1989.

Bowker, John. *God: A Brief History.* New York: DK Publishing Inc., 2002.

Chebel, Malek. *Symbols of Islam.* Paris: Editions Assouline, 1997.

Cohen, Abraham. *Everyman's Talmud: The Major Teachings of the Rabbinic Sages.* New York: Schocken Books, 1995.

Drane, John, ed. *The Great Sayings of Jesus: Proverbs, Parables, and Prayers.* New York: St. Martin's Griffin, 1997.

Eliade, Mircea. *From Primitives to Zen: A Thematic Sourcebook of the History of Religions.* New York: Harper & Row, 1977.

Freedman, David Noel, and Michael J. McClymond, eds. *The Rivers of Paradise: Moses, Buddha, Confucius, Jesus, and Muhammad as Religious Founders.* Grand Rapids, MI: William B. Eerdmans Publishing Company, 2001.

Freke, Timothy. *The Illustrated Book of Sacred Scriptures.* Wheaton, IL: Quest Books, 1998.

Funk, Robert W., Roy W. Hoover, and The Jesus Seminar. *The Five Gospels: The Search for the Authentic Words of Jesus.* New York: HarperSanFrancisco, 1997.

Goerss, John Mark, James R. Pierce, and Chestina Mitchell Archibald, eds. *Divine Inspirations: Pearls of Bible Wisdom from the Old and New Testaments.* Edison, NJ: Castle Books, 1997.

Goring, Rosemary, ed. *Larousse Dictionary of Beliefs and Religions.* New York: Larousse, 1995.

Green, Joey, ed. *Jesus and Moses: The Parallel Sayings.* Berkeley, CA: Seastone, 2002.

The Holy Bible: New International Version. Grand Rapids, MI: Zondervan Publishing House, 1984.

The Interreligious Council of San Diego. *Bridging Our Faiths.* New York/Mahwah, NJ: Paulist Press, 1997.

The Jewish Publication Society. *JPS Hebrew-English Tanakh.* Philadelphia: Jewish Publication Society, 2000.

Jungreis, Esther. *The Committed Life:Principles for Good Living from Our Timeless Past.* New York: HarperCollins Publishers, 1999.

Khalidi, Tarif. *The Muslim Jesus: Sayings and Stories in Islamic Literature.* Cambridge, MA: Harvard University Press, 2001.

Lorie, Peter, and Manuela Dun Mascetti, eds. *The Quotable Spirit: A Treasury of Religious and Spiritual Quotations, from Ancient Times to the 20th Century.* New York: Macmillan, 1996.

Mead, Frank S. *12,000 Inspirational Quotations.* Springfield, MA: Federal Street Press, 2000.

Mitchell, Stephen, ed. *The Essence of Wisdom: Words from the Masters to Illuminate the Spiritual Path.* New York: Broadway Books, 1998.

Moses, Jeffrey. *Oneness: Great Principles Shared By All Religions.* New York: Ballantine Books, 2002.

Novak, Philip. *The World's Wisdom: Sacred Texts of the World's Religions.* Edison, NJ: Castle Books, 1996.

Oman Shannon, Maggie. *The Way We Pray.* Berkeley, CA: Conari Press, 2001.

Parrinder, Geoffrey. *The Routledge Dictionary of Religious & Spiritual Quotations.* London and New York: Routledge, 2000.

———. *World Religions: From Ancient History to the Present.* New York/Bicester, England: Facts on File Publications, 1971.

Perry, Whitall N., ed. *A Treasury of Traditional Wisdom.* Louisville, KY: Fons Vitae, 2000.

Peters, F. E. *Judaism, Christianity, and Islam: The Classical Texts and Their Interpretation, Volume I: From Covenant to Community.* Princeton, NJ: Princeton University Press, 1990.

———. *Judaism, Christianity, and Islam: The Classical Texts and Their Interpretation, Volume II: The Word and the Law and the People of God.* Princeton, NJ: Princeton University Press, 1990.

———. *Judaism, Christianity, and Islam: The Classical Texts and Their Interpretation, Volume III: The Works of the Spirit.* Princeton, NJ: Princeton University Press, 1990.

Renard, John. *The Handy Religion Answer Book.* Detroit: Visible Ink Press, 2002.

———. *Responses to 101 Questions on Islam.* New York/Mahwah, NJ: Paulist Press, 1998.

Smart, Ninian. *The World's Religions.* Cambridge: Cambridge University Press, 1998.

Smith, Huston. *The Illustrated World's Religions: A Guide to Our Wisdom Traditions.* New York: HarperSanFrancisco, 1994.

Smith, Jonathan Z., ed. *The HarperCollins Dictionary of Religion.* New York: HarperSanFrancisco, 1995.

Templeton, Sir John. *Wisdom from World Religions: Pathways Toward Heaven on Earth.* Philadelphia and London: Templeton Foundation Press, 2002.

Tomlinson, Gerald, ed. *Treasury of Religious Quotations.* Englewood Cliffs, NJ: Prentice Hall, 1991.

Wilson, Andrew, ed. *World Scripture: A Comparative Anthology of Sacred Texts.* St. Paul, MN: Paragon House, 1995.

Zerah, Aaron. *The Soul's Almanac: A Year of Interfaith Stories, Prayers, and Wisdom.* New York: Jeremy P. Tarcher/ Putnam, 1998.

magazines

CrossCurrents
www.crosscurrents.org

Hope Magazine
www.hopemag.com

Spirituality and Health
www.spiritualityhealth.com

miscellaneous

CALENDARS

"Inspiration from Great Spiritual Traditions: Judaism, Christianity, Islam," a perpetual calendar (ISBN 0-9666885-0-3) produced by Light & Life, LLC, P.O. Box 60250, Boulder City, NV 89006.

SOFTWARE

"Introspection," a multifaith quotation/journaling software program produced by SoulSoftware, 24360 Old Wagon Road, Escondido, CA 92027; www.soulsoftware.com.

STUDY OPPORTUNITIES / SPIRITUAL DIRECTION

Maggie Oman Shannon
The New Story
415 333-6424
www.thenewstory.com

organizations

Council for a Parliament
of the World's Religions
P.O. Box 1630
Chicago, IL 60690-1630
312 329-2990 • www.cpwr.org

Hope Center
for Interfaith Understanding
North American Branch
c/o William Goldstein
177 Southern Blvd.
Danbury, CT 16810

Interfaith.Org
128 Ft. Washington Ave., #8-1
New York, NY 10032
212 781-3759
www.interfaith.org

International Council
of Christians and Jews
Martin Buber House
Werlestrasse 2, Postfach 1129,
D-64629 Heppenheim, GERMANY
49 6252-5041
www.jcrelations.com/iccj

Project for Joint Standing
Committee of Christians and
the World Muslim Congress
c/o World Council of Churches
150 route de Ferney
PO Box 66
CH-1211 Geneve 2,
SWITZERLAND
22 791-61-11
www.wcc-coe.org

United Communities of Spirit
http://origin.org/ucs

United Religions Initiative
P.O. Box 29242
San Francisco, CA 94129
415 561-2300
www.uri.org

websites

COMPARATIVE RELIGION

www.beliefnet.com

BBC Religion and Ethics site
bbc.co.uk./religion

www.onenessonline.com

www.theharmonyinstitute.org

PEACE ORGANIZATIONS

World Conference on Religion and Peace
www.wcrp.org

www.worldpeace.org

SCRIPTURE REFERENCE

us-israel.org/jsource/Bible/bibletoc.html

religion-cults.com/scriptures.html

www.sacred-texts.com

www.concordance.com

www.ucalgary.ca/~lipton/texts/html